YOUR KNOWLEDGE HAS VALUE

Stephen Gumboh

A Book Analysis of "The Hidden Connections: A Science for Sustainable Living" by Fritjof Capra

GRIN Verlag

Bibliografische Information der Deutschen Nationalbibliothek:

Die Deutsche Bibliothek verzeichnet diese Publikation in der Deutschen National-
bibliografie; detaillierte bibliografische Daten sind im Internet über http://dnb.d-
nb.de/ abrufbar.

Imprint:

Copyright © 2011 GRIN Verlag GmbH
Druck und Bindung: Books on Demand GmbH, Norderstedt Germany
ISBN: 978-3-656-47621-4

This book at GRIN:

http://www.grin.com/en/e-book/231159/a-book-analysis-of-the-hidden-connections-
a-science-for-sustainable-living

GRIN - Your knowledge has value

Der GRIN Verlag publiziert seit 1998 wissenschaftliche Arbeiten von Studenten, Hochschullehrern und anderen Akademikern als eBook und gedrucktes Buch. Die Verlagswebsite www.grin.com ist die ideale Plattform zur Veröffentlichung von Hausarbeiten, Abschlussarbeiten, wissenschaftlichen Aufsätzen, Dissertationen und Fachbüchern.

Visit us on the internet:

http://www.grin.com/

http://www.facebook.com/grincom

http://www.twitter.com/grin_com

The Hidden Connections

Stephen Gumboh

October 2011

Introduction

Capra's new understanding of life is premised on the study of living organisms His understanding is that life "grows inevitably out of increasing complex of cell molecular relationships". It is these relationships that he regards as networks. It is on this premise that he believes that life is a chain of networks. In the book" The Hidden connections", Capra considers these networks as the very essence of life. His view is that every living organism is interdependent and as such co-exists with other organisms for survival. Capra tries to conceptualize this network concept in living systems by presenting a framework integrating the biological, cognitive and social dimensions of life. By integrating these three dimensions of life, Capra tries to justify the essence of the interconnections that equally exist in various human and social organizations. He does so by providing a systematic approach to life's critical issues which continue to have negative impacts on human and social organizations globally. This essay will therefore try to analyse Capra's new understanding of life from a biological, cognitive, and social point of view. Our summary view of Capra's new understanding of life shall then be provided.

The Nature of Life

Capra's biologically view of life starts by his analysis of the cell. Capra emphasizes the point that all living organisms are made of cells and it is only through the cell metabolism processes that living organisms sustain themselves. This is the process of self - generation of living organisms. According to Capra, it is the distinctive individual function of each component in a living organism that makes it genetically possible for it to continually re-generate itself. He however argues that even though cells are made of various constituents, life is not found in these constituents but in the processes that interconnect these constituents. This is the more reason why Capra seems to emphasize the point of interdependence among living organisms. In his view, "no individual living organism can exist in isolation" (Schiffman, 2011). This means that all organisms in whatever form always interact with one another in various ways. Interactions between organisms may be for nourishment, reproduction, or protection and may benefit one of the organisms or both of them. These interactions exist in a form of networks. It is these networks of interconnections among living organisms that Capra refers to as "the hidden connections". It is these interconnections and processes that operate in living organisms that Capra regards as the very essence of life.

When we relate the self – generation of cells in living organisms, we are made to equally agree to Capra's assertion that the same may be applicable to social and organizational systems. However, we are recognizant to the fact that "life is not solely determined genetically but that there are other epigenetic factors that emerge in the process" (Schiffman, 2011). It is these factors, according to Capra, that react to both the physical and chemical contrast of particular environments. What is of essence here is the interaction between the living organisms and their environments. Living organisms by nature are environmentally linked. Our understanding is that living systems are habitant in different environments and their close relationships among themselves result from the environment in which they find themselves. These relationships connect living organisms systematically.

A family is a simplest example of a systematic form of interaction or connections. When we look at an individual person in a family, we see him/ her being surrounded by other family members who are found in his/her environment.Taking a family as a network of living organisms, we can find that all members of the family are interconnect or interact with each other in some way. In any ordinary family, children interact with the father for protection while the mother's connection to the children might be for nourishment. The mother - father relationship could be naturally for family reproduction, nourishment and protection. This implies that every member of the family is connected to someone for the purpose of interdependence or co-existence. This is the survival extinct in living organisms. Any disturbances in these connections may have serious implications on the wellbeing of the family. In instances where the father of the house is the only breadwinner and in the event that he passes on, the family setup may be greatly disturbed eventually leading it to disintegrate. This is usually common in situations where the father in a family is solely dependent upon for every family provision. This is the biological dimension of life where living organism are understood to re-generate or re-create themselves through the network metabolism processes.

Santiago theory of Cognition

However, other than the biological dimension of life, Capra regards the cognitive dimension of life as a unique characteristic of living organisms. In the Wikipedia, "cognition is the scientific term for mental processes". In other words, it is the term that is mostly associated to the mind. It is the mind that is central to information processing and knowledge application in living organisms. The major attribute of the mind is linked to the production and understanding of language which Capra regards as a unique mental function of living organisms. The concept of cognition, in Capra's view, is another key characteristic of all life closely related to the human and social organizations. He argues that the interconnection between cognition and life is one important aspect in living organisms. In his understanding, every sphere of life has a cognitive connection and that all interactions of living systems with their environment are cognitive.

Although Capra prescribes to the Santiago theory of cognition which recognizes mental activity as key to every organizing activity of all living systems, his systemic view of the mind goes beyond the notion that the mind is only a "thinking thing but as a process where the entire structure of the organisation participates".(Schiffman,2011). His view is that living systems, unlike non living systems, use their minds to perceive things. In his view, this "higher-order consciousness or reflective consciousness involves a level of cognitive abstraction that includes the ability to hold mental images. This ability in his view is what gives humans the ability to formulate a value system and act accordingly" (Schiffman, 2011)

Systematic Approach to life

What is prominent in the systematic understanding of life is the exhibition of similar patterns of organisation by different living systems. According to Capra, when this understanding is extended to the social domain, there is every possibility to "apply this knowledge of life's basis patterns and principles of organisation and specifically the understanding of living networks to social reality" (Schiffman, 2011). However, this is not without the understanding that no universal principles of organization can be applicable to all systems in whatever form they can be. These are only assumptions which may only apply to varying situations.

The Social Network

When we come to the issue of social reality, our understanding is that all "social structures are made up of individuals or organizations connected together for a common purpose" (wikipedia.org). What is eminent in all social networks is the applicable mode of communication among individuals in the organisation without putting much pressure on the organization. This is a key factor to understand how far the individual values and beliefs are embraced in these social networks. Capra's point of view is that any "social network can use communication as a way to reproduce itself and its culture and eventually its values and beliefs" (Schiffman, 2011). This communication, according to Capra, takes place in multiple feedback loops.

Our understanding, however, is that not every social network operate the same. Each social network may operate at different levels depending on the nature of relationships that exist. It is the levels in relationships that may determine the possible means on how each network is able to effectively manage all areas of its operations. At a family level, the relationship might be simplistic but when it moves to the level of organization, complexity in relationships might arise depending on the systems at play. The complexities in organisation might give rise to conflicts of interest among individuals in an organization. Capra argues that wherever there is social organisation, there is bound to be conflicts of interest resulting from the desire for power. To him, power is a major influence in the emergence of social structure in the sense that it is this power which provides people with rules of behavior". Notwithstanding this fact, the area of interest is therefore on the nature of these conflicts associated with power. What is obvious to all social networks is that these are just social relationships to which individuals agree to cooperate under certain rules and guidelines, often resulting in social contracts between individuals. To every social contact, there is value attached to it. However, it may be possible that individuals in a social network, though sharing a set of common values might not collectively agree to what suits them best. With these differences in perception, individuals in social networks may differ in many circumstances. This may lead to ideological or physical conflict. This is equally applicable to relationships that are found in organizations.

A thorough examination of interactions in organizations, either informally or formally, may equally prove the fact that conflicts are eminent at every level in the organization due to individual values. In term of power conflict, these are obviously eminent in situations where individuals are more preoccupied in their diversities in thoughts rather focusing themselves to their collective responsibilities. In certain instances, it is the management failure to set rules and procedures accepted at all levels of the organization that may lead to conflicts. Management's favoritism and nepotistic trends, coupled with individuals self – centeredness may be major causes of conflicts in organization. The nature of the social network organization might also be an issue. Our understanding is that open networks are easily acceptable to individuals as these are more set to promote exchange of new ideas and opportunities than closed networks where only set rules and procedures are the norm of the day. This calls for change in organizational setup if the social networks are to be enhanced. However, we are recognizant to the fact that the Change of the status quo in organizations has its own implication on the existing social networks.

Organization and Change

Change in organization may differ according to its nature. In other words, change in organization may be due to process, system, structural or general organizational factors. In all these changes, appropriate strategies may apply. Our understanding of an organization is that it is diverse in nature meaning that it is made up of different patterns of relationships. An organization in its true sense is a fundamental aspect of life where individuals connect together for a common purpose. This agrees with the notion that relationships in organizations exist momentarily between individuals who form the organisation and also between them and those who are in the environment of the organisation. What is core to every organization are the relationships that exist and how these are harmonized at a broader scale without eminent conflicts. Capra brings in the thought of change in organizations as a source of conflict. In his thinking, Capra argues that change is not always associated with conflicts in organizations but that it is "the imposition of this change on individuals they make them to resist" (Schiffman, 2011). He refutes the notion that there is natural aspect to why individuals in organizations resist change. His argument is that the mechanistic thinking of organizations is what presents a hindrance to effective change. His view is that individuals need to change their perception of organizations from being mechanistic to that of communities with collective identities that share common values. He contrasts such organizations to those that exist purely on economic criteria.

By design, organizations are differentiated in line with priorities attached to it. These priorities might be economical or social. To a social organization, his argument is that such organizations do not favour the idea of "controlling organizations through direct interventions but giving impulses rather than instructions" (Schiffman, 2011). His view is that such organizations should not be governed by force but by desires that are collectively acceptable. Instead of using force as means to achieve change, Capra favours the idea of "meaningful disturbances" within an organization as one effective way to achieve structural changes. For this change to be effective and acceptable, individuals to be affected by the perceived change need to be directly involved in the change process. This is with the understanding that Change in organization is not simple and predictable without cooperation from all stakeholders. Our suggested view is that change should encompass the nature of environment in which the change is to take place. This can be illustrated when we consider the change in social organizations to that of the business organizations. Our understanding is that change is not easily attainable in social organizations when compared to those in business organizations. This is due to the fact that business organizations are continuously changing due to the market fluctuations and competition. In order to be viable, businesses require embracing change whenever necessary if they are to keep their clients and increase profitability. The possibility of achieving success change in business organization is high due to the fact that there is less resistance to change in business environments by nature as there are always strategies to enhance the organization's readiness to change. As for social organization, the opposite is found.

Our understanding is that social organizations are found to be rigid to change by their failure embrace change easily due to social implications of change. What is required therefore is for an effective communication strategy to be put in place first as a way to prepare social organizations for the change. This however requires innovative solutions to existing organizational problems by devising a change readiness strategy to assess the change readiness of the organizations. This could be done by analyzing the general "fears" of the individuals in the organisation in order to identify and prioritize the most important issues which might hinder the success of the perceived change. Further, our view is that the organization change readiness may also analyse the behavioral reactions to change by all stakeholders beforehand. Such reactions may include resistance to change characterized by dysfunctional behavior portrayed by anger, suspicion, increased conflict, frustrations, irritation, blaming or being defensive and sometimes even sabotage. This is a natural and inevitable reaction to change and is usually an indication of raised expectations and that individuals are no longer able to operate as expected and are, therefore, uncomfortable and afraid of the unknown. This situation normally occurs where there is not enough information or there is lack of information on the change being proposed.

Our suggested view is that before any perceived change is brought forth, all individuals in the organization need to be sensitized on the change objectives through proper communication methods. It is vital that communication is put as a priority and made a continuous activity in the organization and only evaluated to improve its effectiveness. On the other hand, when an organization sees the need to modify some aspect of its organization and this change demands that individuals should start to act in a different manner, efficient internal communication is necessary. The dynamics of change that occur in organizations demand for an open and flexible organization. Such an organisation requires being open to detect new opportunities in the environment and have the flexibility to adapt in the shorter possible time. This reality requires constant communication within the Organization. It is therefore cardinal that the stakeholder involvement in the change process starts from the beginning of the process for them to buy in and allow for their effective participation in the perceived change. All this is feasible when an enabling environment is provided for their creativity in the change process. Our understanding is that change is an important part of life and as such organisation that do not change to situations extinct.

Economic Globalization and its consequences

Economically, the enabling environment may imply a lot of economic precepts which pertain to varying economies. Capra's starting point in looking at organizations is the admittance that all organizations are socially designed for specific purposes. But the key thing that Capra brings out in his new understanding of life was the issue of the environment in which these organizations operated. Capra's analysis of the current economic environment led him to believe that the current setup of the environment is not conducive to human life. His argument is that current economic environment is life destroying in many ways. His concern was mainly on the practices that pertain in organizations which are putting significant environment strains on the delicate ecosystem. He attributes all these to the financial and material motives of businesses without regard to employees' welfare. According to Capra, "financial and material motives in the long run become a life draining on employees". (Schiffman, 2011). In his view, he regards economic globalization as one of the many strains on the ecosystem. Capra seems not to favour the whole concept of globalization because of its failure to meet its intended objectives and that is to enhance free trade among economies. In his view, globalization brought with it a multitude of interconnected fatal consequences. Capra cites a number of consequences which he considers as having an effect in many economies such as social disintegration and a breakdown of democracy. Further, he argues that the same globalization has resulted in rapid and extensive deterioration of the environment. He also attributes globalization to the spread of diseases and the increase in poverty levels and alienation. Our fair comment on the breakdown of democracy in economies hinges on behaviors, practices and norms that define the ability of people to govern themselves. Our understanding of democracy is that it is not static. It moves with the times and cannot be automated. Democracy hinges on proper principles and procedures for it to run efficiently. In a democracy, the importance point to note is that all economies comprises a great diversity of interests and individuals and deserve to have their views respected. And the voices of democracy include not only those of the government and its external cooperating partners but also those of opposite but indigenous views from local trade unions, organized interest groups, the media ,religious leaders and so on and so forth.

All these need to be provided the opportunity to indigenously participate effectively in the democratic process.

However, it is quite acceptable to a certain level to note the global economic trends that have, over the past periods, exerted pressures on rising unemployment and widening social inequalities in many developing economies. Notwithstanding the above, we need to note despite these challenges; no single economy can provide solutions to the challenges cited above without international cooperation. With the full knowledge that all economies are experiencing individual economic challenges, it is also important to suggest that a common global agenda is devised to meet these challenges head – on without undue pressures on smaller economies. Such pressures if allowed would make the whole essence of globalization a futile concept. Capra suggests that for globalization to have positive meaning to small economies, there is need to re- organize the whole global economy.

Biotechnology

As for global effects on the environment, and the spread of diseases, Capra attributes this to the advert of biotechnology. This arise from the period of the green revolution where its proponents promised positive effects of genetically engineered commodities and new insect resistant crop varieties and long life fresh fruits. It is in the period of the green revolution that saw the introduction of chemical fertilizers and pesticides into agriculture and practice of single crop monoculture into the business of agriculture. Capra's argument on practices of the green revolution is their long term effects on human health as well as on the ecosystems. This is contrarily to the green revolution proponents who argued that the green revolution had its positive impacts both humanly and environmentally. Their argument is that with the coming of the green revolution, a number of positive effects were achieved such as the increase of crop production and yield due to better scientific methods applied coupled with the development of new seed varieties with better yield and disease fighting capabilities. However these were over-shouldered by the long run negative impacts of the green revolution. Health-wise, the critics of the green revolution argues that excessive use of chemicals in water had a long term effect on human and animal life due to its contamination effects on water. Further, it is argued that with the heavy use of chemical pesticides, insecticides and fertilizers, there has being a long term loss of birds and friendly insects ecologically essential to the environment. Worse of all, the issue of degradation of the environment is greatly attributed to the green revolution practices. It is argued that the green revolution brought about the degradation of land in the form of land quality and yield. This is attributable to the change in land use pattern. The argument on the utilization of heavy chemical fertilizer inputs is that it had a long term effect on the land carbon material. Further still, the introduction of high yielding seed varieties equally had its own long term genetic effects. In addition, there is the view that as a result of the increase in the use of agrochemical based pesticides and weed control methods; these have had an effect on the environment.

An ecological Alternative

It is from this understanding that Capra tries to provide an ecological alternative to address the long term effects of the green revolution. Capra considers organic farming as an ecological alternative to the adverse effects of the green revolution. His view is that "organic farming preserves and sustains the ecological cycles by integrating biological processes into food production" (Schiffman, 2011). Further, he argues that with organic farming, there is the possibility of the soil to increase its carbon content. It is this increase in the soil's carbon content that, in his view, could help in reducing global warming. This is the view that is supported by proponents of organic farming. They cite a number of advantages associated to organic farming which they regard as a counterbalance to the effects of the green revolution. Proponents of organic farming argue that with organic farming, the life of the soil is improved and allowing plants to have direct access to soil nutrients. It is further argued that food organically grown has superior mineral content causing it to increase its nutritional value. Additionally, there is the notion that plants organically grown in properly balanced soil are resistant to most diseases and insect pests and therefore remain healthy for a long time. The resistance of organic crops to pests and the diseases give an advantage to farmers to save significantly on insecticides, fungicides and other pesticides. The less usage of these health harming chemicals makes organic food to be free from contamination. As for treatment of weeds in organic farming, unlike in the green revolution, these are treated as nature's remedy to restore soil fertility. The argument is weeds do not provide any harm to healthy organic crops which are able to sustain themselves due to their resistance. The other significance of organically grown plants is that there are drought resistant. On the environment, proponents of organic farming argue that it is very beneficial to food production in the sense that it does not have a negative effect on the environment. Climate wise, it is argued that organic farming is significant in that it produces less greenhouse gas emissions due its low input needs of naturally derived substances. This is one aspect that makes organic farming to be an ideal ecological alternative. However, caution is given on the possibility of some incidences of diseases such as cancer occurring which are greatly associated with the exposure to toxic chemicals in organic farming. Despite all these advantages of organic farming as an ecological alternative, it still remains for its proponents and other stakeholders to put in interventions to propagate it to a large extent. This is where Capra sees the significant role of non-government organizations (NGOs) in this area.

The role of NGOs

According to Capra all this can be attainable if only people can change the perception in the way they look at things economically and environmentally. Once this is realized, it is only when the significant of the eco - designed alternatives could be appreciated. Capra suggests that instead of looking to Government to advocate for this change in perception, it is better to look to NGOs. His argument is that Government cannot be in a position to advocate for change because of their direct connection to the stakeholder businesses and industries. Capra favours the idea of NGOs as channels of change. His view is that NGOs being more grassroot in their operations are more linked to society. In this way they fit in well as agents of change. By their position in society, there are able to exert a lot of influence to the life of societies in which they serve. According to Capra, NGOs are a powerful network that cuts across many big and smaller organizations. With this in mind, Capra advances his new understanding of life by advocating for NGOs as a new civil society which is more powerful to influence change. In his mind, NGOs are an effective tool of communication and as the way for the future. His understanding is that NGOs by their design are oriented to perform varying global activities in many different spheres of life, be it socially or culturally. The only possible way to achieve this position is for NGOs to get together and enhance their networking to the global level. Our support of this notion is based on our understanding that a united NGO civil society has the ability to get together and advance their cause for change wherever necessary. Further, it is cost saving to have NGOs interlinked to enhance their impact as impact as policy negotiators and advocating agencies. An effective networking among NGOs, in our view, is vital for information sharing and knowledge transfers and also as a means to influence decision-making at all levels requiring social change. Social change, as it is understood, is communication based and any form of interaction is all about communication. We are however recognizant to the fact of the heterogeneity of those NGOs which could make it difficult for them to easily corroborate on matters of change. The main difficult perceived is to do with failures to reach consensus on the implication of the perceived change. What is factual is that these NGOs are created for varying purposes and as such might be more inclined to their mandated activities than to trend on areas of less interest. However, it is important to note that every networking can only be actively participative when all the partners cooperate in the network process. This is the only sure way that can make networking to be effective and sustainable.

Summary

In summary, we may conclude to say that Capra's new understanding of life brings with it a lot of human and organizational implications. These implications may hinge on social, cultural and religious aspects of life. However we agree with Capra in his argument for organizations to take a systematic approach to new ways of doing business. There is need to create value systems in organizations. We agree to the notion that humans in very situation have value systems which play a major role in how they conduct themselves in varying situations. Further it is also our opinionated idea that as we look ahead to a socially and economically viable society, we need to urgently address the challenges pointed out above. We equally agree with Capra on the need to strive towards a sustainable society by redesigning technologies and social institutions without undue distraction of our natural environment. However, we are recognizant to the fact that all these challenges may be difficult to attain without political will at a global level.

Although we agree in principle to most of Capra's views of life, it is our feeling, however, that these views may be situational and not binding to every human and organization activity of life. We however note the issue of networking to be very crucial but need serious consideration at every level of activity. What is obvious is that Capra's scientific background play a major influence to his thinking in his book "The Hidden connections". However, we are recognizant to the fact that not only does the thinking in the book influence the direction of the analysis, but by exploring varying sources of the book, some aspects of the book might have been misconstrued. Our view is that the book is not scientifically oriented to the level of a non - scientific mind and as such cannot be easily comprehended. Notwithstanding this fact, the overall scope of the book seems to cater for all intellectual areas of life. It is masterpiece of its kind.

References

Capra Fritjof, 2002, The Hidden Connections: A Science for Sustainable Living, Anchor Books, Random House, Inc, New York

Brodsky Bart, 2004, Exploring the Hidden Connections, Interview with Fritjof Capra,

Schiffman, Darian, 2011, a video conference presentation on Capra's book "Hidden connections - A science for sustainable living, Atlantic International University.